I0489820

Title: "Mastering Marketing Strategies in FMCG"

This book, along with its contents encompassing text, illustrations, images, diagrams, and other creative elements, is the exclusive property of FAISAL JAMIL and is safeguarded by copyright law.

While efforts have been made to ensure accuracy and reliability, FAISAL JAMIL does not guarantee the completeness or suitability of the information. Readers are responsible for evaluating and using the content judiciously.

FAISAL JAMIL reserves the right to make changes, updates, or corrections to the book without prior notice. Inclusion of third-party materials or references does not imply

Warm regards,

FAISAL JAMIL

I Always Give's Free Copies Need Your Feedback And

Reviews Keeps In Touch!

http://www.amazon.com/author/faisal.jamil

Email: faisaljamilauthor@gmail.com

About the author

Certainly! Faisal Jamil is a multifaceted individual with a diverse set of skills and experiences. With a strong foundation in computer knowledge since childhood, he has developed a deep understanding of technology that informs his work as a content writer. Faisal also possesses digital skills, which further enhance his abilities in various digital platforms and technologies.

Beyond his professional endeavors, Faisal Jamil has also excelled in the martial arts, particularly Shotokan Karate, where he achieved the prestigious rank of first Dan black belt. This achievement speaks to his dedication, discipline, and commitment to personal growth and mastery.

In his professional life, Faisal Jamil has carved out a successful career in sales management within the Fast Moving Consumer Goods (FMCG) sector. His roles in various FMCG companies have honed his skills in strategic planning, team leadership, and business development. Faisal's ability to drive sales and achieve targets has been instrumental in his career progression, showcasing his talent for identifying opportunities and delivering results.

Faisal Jamil is also deeply interested in business investment strategies, planning, and execution. His understanding of these areas has been key to his success in the business world, allowing him to make informed decisions and implement effective strategies. His ability to navigate the complexities of investment planning and execution has set him apart as a strategic thinker and a valuable asset in any business endeavor.

Overall, Faisal Jamil is a dynamic individual who combines his passion for technology, martial arts, sales management, digital skills, and business investment strategies to achieve success in diverse fields. His journey is a testament to his versatility, resilience, and continuous pursuit of excellence.

Yours Sincerely

FAISAL JAMIL

I Always Give's Free Copies Need Your Feedback And

Reviews Keeps In Touch!

https://www.amazon.com/author/faisal.jamil

Email: faisaljamilauthor@gmail.com

MASTERING
MARKETING STRATEGIES IN
FMCG

Table of Content

INTRODUCTION

Welcome to "Mastering Marketing Strategies in FMCG," a comprehensive guide designed to navigate the fast-paced and competitive world of Fast-Moving Consumer Goods (FMCG). Whether you're a seasoned marketing professional, an entrepreneur looking to break into the FMCG market, or a student aspiring to build a career in this dynamic industry, this book is tailored to provide you with the knowledge and strategies needed to excel.

Why FMCG? The FMCG sector, encompassing everyday items such as food, beverages, toiletries, and other consumer goods, is a unique market characterized by high sales volumes and low-profit margins. Its fast-paced nature demands constant innovation and adaptability. With consumers increasingly driven by convenience, price sensitivity, and brand loyalty, mastering the intricacies of

FMCG marketing is essential for achieving sustained growth and market leadership.

What to Expect This book is divided into five comprehensive chapters, each focusing on critical aspects of FMCG marketing:

Understanding the FMCG Landscape: We begin with an exploration of the fundamental dynamics of the FMCG market. You'll gain insights into consumer behavior, the impact of trends like sustainability and digital transformation, and learn techniques for market segmentation and competitive analysis.

Brand Building and Management: Building a strong brand is crucial in the FMCG sector. This chapter covers the creation and maintenance of brand identity and equity, integrated marketing communications, and the strategic use of both traditional and digital marketing channels, including influencer marketing.

Product and Pricing Strategies: Successful FMCG companies are those that innovate continually. This chapter delves into product lifecycle management, the importance of innovation, and various pricing strategies. You'll also learn about distribution and supply chain management, with a focus on e-commerce and omnichannel approaches.

Consumer Engagement and Retention: Engaging and retaining consumers is vital for long-term success. We explore customer experience management, loyalty programs, and CRM systems, emphasizing the role of feedback and continuous improvement.

Sustainability and Future Trends: The final chapter addresses the increasing importance of sustainability in FMCG marketing. We discuss strategies for environmental and social responsibility, the need for agility and technological innovation, and provide insights into future consumer trends and strategic planning.

Our Approach This book is designed to be practical and actionable. Through real-world examples, case studies, and detailed explanations, you'll gain a thorough understanding of how to apply these strategies in your own context. Each chapter builds on the previous one, creating a holistic framework for mastering FMCG marketing.

Who Should Read This Book? "Mastering Marketing Strategies in FMCG" is ideal for:

Marketing professionals seeking to deepen their knowledge and stay ahead in a competitive market.

Entrepreneurs and business owners aiming to launch or grow their FMCG ventures.

Students and academics studying marketing, business, or related fields.

Anyone interested in understanding the intricacies of the FMCG sector and its marketing strategies.

We invite you to embark on this journey through the dynamic world of FMCG marketing. By mastering the strategies outlined in this book, you'll be well-equipped to navigate the challenges and seize the opportunities that this vibrant industry offers.

Let's get started!

Chapter 1

Understanding the FMCG Landscape

1.1 The Dynamics of FMCG Markets

Market Characteristics The FMCG market is characterized by its rapid pace, large volume sales, and low profit margins. Products in this sector are typically sold quickly and at relatively low cost. Companies must efficiently manage high turnover rates and balance cost control with the need to maintain quality.

Consumer Behavior Consumer purchasing habits in FMCG are heavily influenced by convenience, price, and brand loyalty. Shoppers often seek products that are easily accessible and offer good value for money. Understanding the drivers behind these purchasing decisions is crucial for crafting effective marketing strategies.

Trends and Innovations

Current trends in FMCG include a strong emphasis on sustainability, with consumers favoring eco-friendly products and packaging. Health-conscious products are also on the rise, reflecting growing consumer awareness of health and wellness. Additionally, digital transformation is reshaping the FMCG landscape, with e-commerce and digital marketing becoming increasingly important.

1.2 Market Segmentation and Targeting

Segmentation Techniques Market segmentation involves dividing the market into distinct groups of consumers with similar needs or characteristics. This can be done based on:

Demographics: Age, gender, income, education, etc.

Psychographics: Lifestyle, values, interests.

Geography: Location-based segmentation.

Behavior: Purchasing habits, brand loyalty, usage rates.

Targeting Strategies After segmentation, the next step is targeting, which involves selecting the most attractive segments to focus marketing efforts on. Strategies include:

Mass Marketing: Targeting the entire market with a single marketing mix.

Differentiated Marketing: Targeting several market segments with a distinct marketing mix for each.

Niche Marketing: Concentrating efforts on a small, specialized segment.

Positioning Positioning is about creating a unique image of the product in the consumer's mind. Effective positioning requires:

Identifying unique selling propositions (USPs).

Communicating the benefits that differentiate the product from competitors.

Ensuring consistency in messaging across all marketing channels.

1.3 Competitive Analysis

Identifying Competitors In the FMCG sector, it's vital to identify both direct competitors (those offering similar products) and indirect competitors (those offering substitute products). Understanding the competitive landscape helps in crafting strategies that address competitive pressures.

Analyzing Competitor Strategies Analyzing competitors involves evaluating their strengths, weaknesses, opportunities, and threats (SWOT analysis). Key aspects to consider include:

Product offerings: Range, quality, and innovation.

Pricing strategies: Competitive pricing, discount policies.

Distribution channels: Reach and efficiency.

Marketing efforts: Advertising, promotions, and brand presence.

Strategic Planning To outperform competitors, companies must develop strategic plans that leverage their unique selling propositions (USPs). This includes:

Innovative product development: Staying ahead through constant innovation.

Effective marketing campaigns: Creating impactful advertising and promotions.

Operational efficiency: Streamlining supply chains and reducing costs to offer competitive pricing.

In summary, Chapter 1 of "Mastering Marketing Strategies in FMCG" provides a comprehensive overview of the FMCG market dynamics, emphasizing the importance of understanding market characteristics, consumer behavior, current trends, segmentation and targeting strategies, and competitive analysis. These foundational concepts set the stage for developing effective marketing strategies in the FMCG sector.

Chapter 2

Brand Building and Management

2.1 Brand Identity and Equity

Creating a Brand Identity Developing a compelling brand identity is a crucial step in establishing a strong presence in the FMCG market. The process involves:

Logo Design: A visually appealing logo that represents the brand's values and mission.

Tagline: A memorable and succinct tagline that encapsulates the brand's essence.

Brand Voice: Consistent tone and style of communication that aligns with the brand's personality, whether it's formal, friendly, humorous, or authoritative.

A strong brand identity helps distinguish a brand from its competitors and creates an emotional connection with consumers.

Building Brand Equity Brand equity refers to the value a brand adds to a product. Strategies to build brand equity include:

Customer Experiences: Delivering exceptional customer experiences through quality products and excellent service.

Quality Assurance: Ensuring consistent product quality to build trust and reliability.

Consistent Messaging: Maintaining uniformity in brand messaging across all platforms to reinforce the brand's values and promises.

Effective brand equity leads to greater customer loyalty, the ability to charge premium prices, and increased market share.

Brand Loyalty Fostering brand loyalty is essential for long-term success in the FMCG sector. Techniques to achieve this include:

Loyalty Programs: Rewarding repeat customers with points, discounts, and exclusive offers.

Engagement: Regularly engaging with customers through social media, newsletters, and events to build a community around the brand.

Personalization: Offering personalized experiences and products tailored to individual customer preferences.

Brand loyalty results in repeat purchases, positive word-of-mouth, and a strong brand reputation.

2.2 Marketing Communication Strategies

Integrated Marketing Communications (IMC) IMC involves combining traditional and digital marketing channels to deliver a cohesive and consistent message. This approach ensures that all marketing efforts are aligned and reinforce each other. Key components of IMC include:

Traditional Media: Utilizing TV, radio, and print media for broad reach and brand visibility.

Digital Media: Leveraging online platforms, including social media, email, and websites, for targeted and interactive marketing.

A well-executed IMC strategy enhances brand recall and drives consumer action.

Advertising and Promotions Effective advertising and promotional strategies are vital for capturing consumer attention and driving sales. Techniques include:

TV and Radio Ads: High-impact visual and audio ads that reach a wide audience.

Print Advertising: Targeted ads in newspapers, magazines, and outdoor billboards.

Online Advertising: Utilizing search engine marketing (SEM), display ads, and social media ads for precise targeting.

Sales Promotions: Short-term incentives like discounts, coupons, and buy-one-get-one-free offers to stimulate immediate purchases.

These strategies help create awareness, generate interest, and encourage trial and repeat purchases.

Public Relations and Sponsorships PR and sponsorships play a critical role in enhancing brand visibility and credibility. Approaches include:

Media Relations: Building relationships with journalists and influencers to secure positive media coverage.

Event Sponsorships: Sponsoring events that align with the brand's values and target audience to increase exposure and goodwill.

Community Engagement: Participating in or supporting community initiatives to build a positive brand image.

Effective PR and sponsorships help create a favorable public perception and strengthen the brand's reputation.

2.3 Digital and Social Media Marketing

Digital Marketing Tactics Digital marketing is essential for reaching and engaging today's connected consumers. Key tactics include:

SEO (Search Engine Optimization): Optimizing website content to rank higher in search engine results and attract organic traffic.

SEM (Search Engine Marketing): Using paid search ads to appear at the top of search engine results for relevant keywords.

Email Marketing: Sending targeted and personalized email campaigns to nurture leads and retain customers.

Content Marketing: Creating valuable and relevant content, such as blogs, videos, and infographics, to attract and engage the target audience.

Digital marketing tactics help build an online presence, drive traffic, and convert visitors into customers.

Social Media Strategies Social media is a powerful tool for engaging with consumers and building brand loyalty. Best practices include:

Platform Selection: Choosing the right platforms (e.g., Facebook, Instagram, TikTok) based on the target audience's preferences.

Content Creation: Developing engaging content, including images, videos, stories, and live streams, to capture audience interest.

Engagement: Actively interacting with followers through comments, messages, and social media contests to foster a sense of community.

A strong social media strategy enhances brand visibility and encourages user-generated content and word-of-mouth marketing.

Influencer Marketing Collaborating with influencers can significantly amplify a brand's reach and credibility. Steps to leverage influencer marketing include:

Identifying Relevant Influencers: Finding influencers whose audience aligns with the brand's target market.

Creating Authentic Partnerships: Working with influencers to create genuine and relatable content that showcases the brand's products.

Measuring Impact: Tracking key metrics such as engagement, reach, and conversions to evaluate the effectiveness of influencer campaigns.

Influencer marketing can drive brand awareness, credibility, and conversions by leveraging the trust and influence of popular personalities.

Chapter 3

Product and Pricing Strategies

3.1 Product Development and Innovation

Product Lifecycle Management Understanding the product lifecycle is crucial for effective management. The lifecycle includes four stages:

Introduction: At this stage, products are launched into the market. Strategies focus on creating awareness and stimulating demand through marketing and promotions.

Growth: As products gain acceptance, the focus shifts to increasing market share. Strategies include enhancing distribution, improving product features, and competitive pricing.

Maturity: During maturity, market saturation occurs. Strategies involve differentiating the product, finding new market segments, and enhancing customer loyalty.

Decline: In the decline stage, sales decrease. Strategies may include reducing costs, discontinuing the product, or rejuvenating it through innovation.

Innovation in FMCG Innovation is vital in FMCG to meet evolving consumer needs and stay ahead of competitors. Key aspects include:

Importance of Innovation: Keeps the product lineup fresh, meets changing consumer preferences, and differentiates from competitors.

Fostering a Culture of Innovation: Encouraging creativity within teams, investing in R&D, and staying informed about market trends.

Techniques for Innovation: Using consumer insights, adopting new technologies, and collaborating with external partners for fresh ideas.

Portfolio Management Managing a diverse product portfolio involves balancing various products to maximize profitability and market presence. Strategies include:

Analyzing Product Performance: Regularly reviewing the performance of each product using metrics like sales, market share, and profitability.

Portfolio Optimization: Identifying underperforming products for improvement or discontinuation and investing in high-potential products.

Diversification: Expanding the product range to include new categories or markets to spread risk and increase revenue streams.

3.2 Pricing Strategies

Pricing Models Choosing the right pricing model is critical for balancing profitability and competitiveness. Common models include:

Cost-Plus Pricing: Adding a fixed percentage markup to the cost of production. Simple but may not reflect market conditions.

Value-Based Pricing: Setting prices based on the perceived value to the customer. Requires understanding customer perceptions and market positioning.

Competition-Based Pricing: Setting prices based on competitors' strategies. Useful in highly competitive markets but requires continuous monitoring.

Price Optimization Optimizing pricing strategies involves fine-tuning prices to achieve business objectives. Techniques include:

Dynamic Pricing: Adjusting prices based on real-time demand, competition, and other factors.

Price Elasticity Analysis: Understanding how changes in price affect demand to set optimal price points.

Promotional Pricing: Using temporary price reductions, discounts, and special offers to drive short-term sales and boost customer acquisition.

Promotional Pricing Promotional pricing is an effective way to stimulate sales and increase market share. Strategies include:

Discounts: Offering temporary price reductions to attract new customers or clear inventory.

Bundling: Combining products at a reduced price to increase perceived value and encourage higher purchases.

Loyalty Programs: Providing special offers and discounts to repeat customers to foster loyalty and increase lifetime value.

3.3 Distribution and Supply Chain Management

Distribution Channels Effective distribution ensures products reach consumers efficiently and conveniently. Channels include:

Direct Distribution: Selling directly to consumers through company-owned stores, websites, or direct sales teams. Provides greater control but can be costly.

Indirect Distribution: Using intermediaries like wholesalers, retailers, and distributors to reach a wider audience. Cost-effective but less control over the customer experience.

Supply Chain Optimization Optimizing the supply chain is essential for reducing costs and improving service levels. Strategies involve:

Process Streamlining: Simplifying and automating processes to increase efficiency and reduce errors.

Inventory Management: Using techniques like Just-In-Time (JIT) to minimize inventory costs while ensuring availability.

Supplier Relationships: Building strong relationships with suppliers to ensure quality, reliability, and favorable terms.

E-commerce and Omnichannel Strategies Integrating online and offline channels is critical for providing a seamless shopping experience. Approaches include:

E-commerce Platforms: Developing user-friendly online stores with efficient order processing and delivery.

Omnichannel Integration: Ensuring consistent pricing, promotions, and product availability across all channels.

Click-and-Collect: Allowing customers to order online and pick up in-store, combining the convenience of online shopping with the immediacy of in-store pickup.

Chapter 4

Consumer Engagement and Retention

4.1 Customer Experience Management

Customer Journey Mapping Customer journey mapping involves understanding and visualizing the steps a customer takes from initial awareness to post-purchase interaction. Techniques for effective journey mapping include:

Identifying Touchpoints: Listing all the points where customers interact with the brand, such as website visits, in-store experiences, customer service interactions, and social media engagement.

Creating Personas: Developing detailed customer personas to represent different segments of the target audience. This helps in understanding their needs, motivations, and pain points.

Mapping Stages: Dividing the journey into stages such as awareness, consideration, purchase, retention, and advocacy. Each stage should highlight the customer's goals, actions, and emotions.

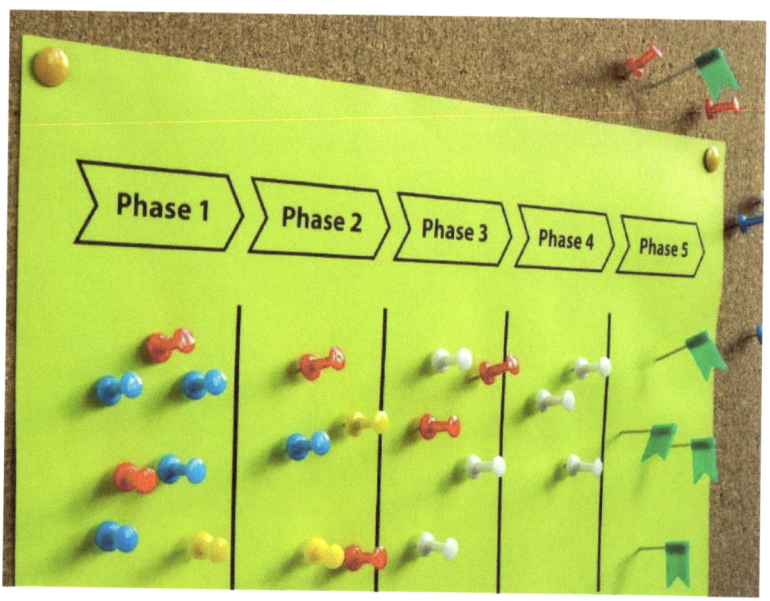

Identifying Pain Points: Analyzing each touchpoint to identify potential obstacles and areas for improvement. This helps in enhancing the overall customer experience.

Personalization Personalization involves using data and analytics to tailor experiences and recommendations to individual customers. Key strategies include:

Data Collection: Gathering data from various sources, including purchase history, browsing behavior, and customer preferences.

Segmentation: Segmenting customers based on their behavior and preferences to deliver more relevant content and offers.

Personalized Communication: Using personalized emails, product recommendations, and targeted advertisements to engage customers effectively.

Real-Time Personalization: Implementing real-time personalization on websites and apps to dynamically change content based on customer behavior.

Customer Service Excellence Providing exceptional customer service is crucial for enhancing satisfaction and loyalty. Strategies include:

Training Staff: Ensuring that customer service teams are well-trained, knowledgeable, and equipped to handle various customer queries and issues.

Multichannel Support: Offering support through multiple channels, including phone, email, live chat, and social media, to provide convenience and accessibility.

Proactive Service: Anticipating customer needs and addressing potential issues before they escalate. This can include sending reminders, updates, and follow-ups.

Feedback Loop: Encouraging customers to provide feedback on their service experience and using this information to make continuous improvements.

4.2 Loyalty Programs and CRM

Designing Loyalty Programs Effective loyalty programs incentivize repeat purchases and brand advocacy. Steps to create successful programs include:

Defining Objectives: Setting clear goals for the loyalty program, such as increasing repeat purchases, enhancing customer engagement, or boosting brand advocacy.

Reward Structure: Designing a reward structure that offers valuable and attainable rewards. This can include points-based systems, tiered memberships, or exclusive perks.

Personalization: Tailoring rewards and offers based on customer preferences and purchase history to increase relevance and engagement.

Promotion and Communication: Actively promoting the loyalty program through various channels and ensuring customers are aware of the benefits and how to participate.

Customer Relationship Management (CRM) Implementing CRM systems helps manage customer interactions and data effectively. Key aspects include:

Data Integration: Integrating data from various touchpoints to create a unified view of each customer.

Automation: Using CRM tools to automate repetitive tasks such as sending follow-up emails, updating customer records, and segmenting customers.

Analytics: Leveraging CRM analytics to gain insights into customer behavior, preferences, and trends.

Customer Segmentation: Segmenting customers based on their behavior and preferences to deliver more targeted and personalized experiences.

Measuring Loyalty Measuring the success of loyalty programs and retention efforts involves tracking key metrics and KPIs, such as:

Customer Retention Rate: The percentage of customers who continue to purchase from the brand over a specific period.

Customer Lifetime Value (CLV): The total revenue a customer is expected to generate throughout their relationship with the brand.

Net Promoter Score (NPS): A measure of customer satisfaction and loyalty based on the likelihood of customers recommending the brand to others.

Redemption Rate: The percentage of loyalty program members who redeem rewards, indicating engagement and program effectiveness.

4.3 Feedback and Continuous Improvement

Collecting Customer Feedback Gathering customer feedback is essential for understanding their needs and improving offerings. Methods include:

Surveys: Conducting online or in-store surveys to gather feedback on specific aspects of the customer experience.

Reviews and Ratings: Encouraging customers to leave reviews and ratings on websites, social media, and third-party platforms.

Social Listening: Monitoring social media channels for mentions, comments, and feedback about the brand.

Focus Groups: Organizing focus groups to gain in-depth insights into customer opinions and preferences.

Analyzing Feedback Analyzing customer feedback helps identify areas for improvement and innovation. Techniques include:

Sentiment Analysis: Using tools to analyze the sentiment of customer feedback and identify positive, neutral, or negative sentiments.

Trend Analysis: Identifying common themes and trends in customer feedback to understand recurring issues and opportunities.

Root Cause Analysis: Investigating the underlying causes of negative feedback to address the root issues effectively.

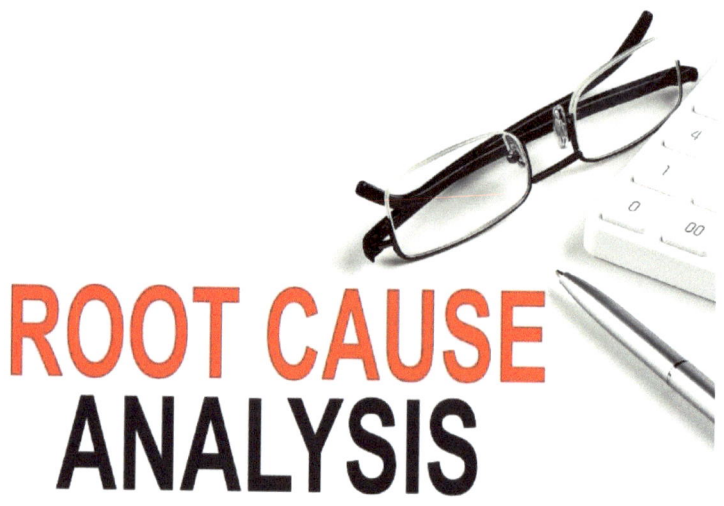

Implementing Changes Implementing changes based on customer feedback involves a structured process to ensure continuous improvement. Steps include:

Prioritization: Prioritizing feedback based on its impact on customer satisfaction and business goals.

Action Plans: Developing action plans to address the identified issues and improve the customer experience.

Communication: Communicating changes and improvements to customers to show that their feedback is valued and acted upon.

Monitoring and Evaluation: Continuously monitoring the impact of implemented changes and making further adjustments as needed.

Chapter 5

Sustainability and Future Trends

5.1 Sustainable Marketing Practices

Environmental Responsibility In the FMCG sector, reducing environmental impact is crucial for long-term sustainability. Strategies include:

Sustainable Sourcing: Procuring raw materials from sustainable sources to minimize environmental degradation. This includes using renewable resources and ensuring fair labor practices.

Eco-friendly Packaging: Developing packaging solutions that reduce waste, are biodegradable, recyclable, or made from recycled materials.

Green Operations: Implementing energy-efficient processes, reducing carbon footprints, and minimizing waste throughout the supply chain. This can involve optimizing logistics to reduce emissions and investing in renewable energy sources.

Social Responsibility Supporting social causes and ethical practices enhances brand reputation and aligns with consumer values. Initiatives include:

Fair Trade Practices: Ensuring fair wages and working conditions for suppliers and workers in the supply chain.

Community Engagement: Investing in local communities through educational programs, health initiatives, and economic support.

Ethical Marketing: Promoting products transparently, avoiding misleading claims, and ensuring advertising aligns with ethical standards.

Communicating Sustainability Effectively communicating sustainability efforts to consumers builds trust and loyalty. Approaches include:

Transparency: Providing clear and honest information about sustainability practices, sourcing, and product ingredients.

Storytelling: Using storytelling to share the brand's journey towards sustainability, including challenges and successes.

Certifications and Labels: Displaying recognized sustainability certifications (e.g., Fair Trade, Organic, Carbon Neutral) to provide credibility and assurance to consumers.

5.2 Adapting to Market Changes

Agility in FMCG Agility is critical in the fast-paced FMCG sector to respond swiftly to market changes and consumer trends. Key aspects include:

Flexible Operations: Implementing flexible manufacturing and supply chain processes that can quickly adapt to changes in demand or disruptions.

Rapid Innovation: Fostering a culture of innovation that encourages rapid development and testing of new products.

Responsive Marketing: Utilizing real-time data to adjust marketing strategies and campaigns in response to emerging trends and consumer behavior.

Technology and Innovation Leveraging technology drives innovation and efficiency in the FMCG sector. Key technologies include:

Artificial Intelligence (AI): Using AI for predictive analytics, personalized marketing, and optimizing supply chain operations.

Internet of Things (IoT): Implementing IoT devices for real-time monitoring and automation of production and logistics.

Blockchain: Enhancing transparency and traceability in the supply chain with blockchain technology, ensuring authenticity and ethical sourcing.

Future Consumer Trends Staying ahead of future consumer trends is vital for maintaining relevance and competitiveness. Predictions include:

Health and Wellness: Increasing demand for healthier, organic, and functional foods driven by health-conscious consumers.

Digital Engagement: Growing importance of digital and mobile platforms for consumer engagement and e-commerce.

Sustainability: Continued emphasis on sustainability, with consumers prioritizing brands that demonstrate environmental and social responsibility.

5.3 Strategic Planning for the Future

Long-term Strategic Planning Developing long-term strategies ensures sustained growth and competitiveness. Steps include:

Vision and Goals: Establishing a clear vision and long-term goals aligned with market opportunities and consumer needs.

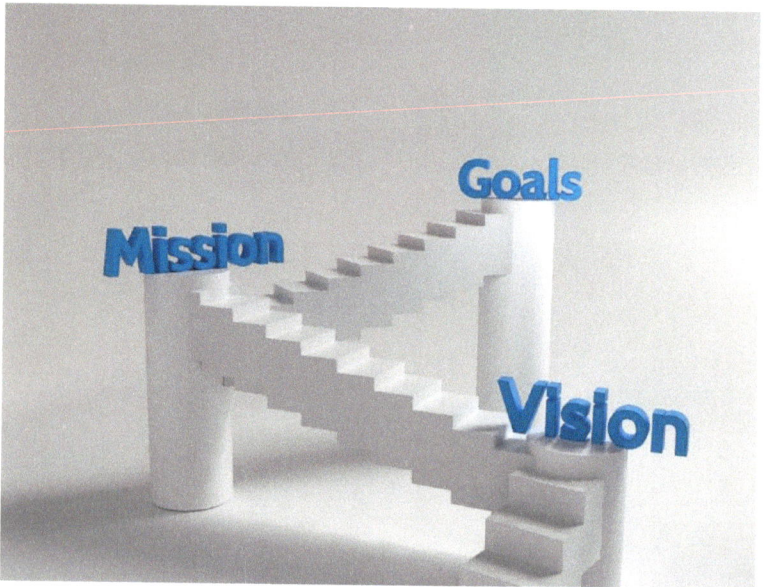

Market Analysis: Conducting thorough market analysis to identify growth opportunities, emerging trends, and potential challenges.

Resource Allocation: Allocating resources effectively to prioritize key initiatives and investments that drive long-term value.

Scenario Planning Scenario planning helps anticipate and prepare for potential market changes. Techniques include:

Identifying Key Drivers: Recognizing key drivers of change such as economic conditions, technological advancements, and regulatory changes.

Developing Scenarios: Creating multiple scenarios based on different assumptions about the future to explore various outcomes.

Strategic Response: Formulating strategic responses for each scenario to ensure readiness and flexibility in the face of uncertainty.

Continuous Learning and Adaptation Continuous learning and adaptation are essential in a rapidly evolving industry. Strategies include:

Industry Benchmarking: Regularly benchmarking against industry standards and best practices to identify areas for improvement.

Feedback Loops: Establishing feedback loops with customers, employees, and partners to continuously gather insights and improve processes.

Training and Development: Investing in ongoing training and development programs to keep the workforce updated with the latest skills and knowledge.

The End!

Needs Your Positive Review & Feedback!

www.ingramcontent.com/pod-product-compliance
Lightning Source LLC
Chambersburg PA
CBHW040758240526
45474CB00008B/103

9 798328 383509